Ages 7-9

KV-495-941

# Music Works

## A complete resource pack for primary music

## Carol Donaldson    Carmel McCourt

## Acknowledgements

Thanks to Oliver McCourt for performing the rap on 'Bully'.

Thanks to Felix Donaldson, Isla Donaldson, Leah Molyneux and Saskia Speed for performing the rap on 'Senua da Dende'.

© 2006 Folens Limited, on behalf of the authors.

United Kingdom: Folens Publishers, Apex Business Centre, Boscombe Road, Dunstable, LU5 4RL. Email: folens@folens.com

Ireland: Folens Publishers, Greenhills Road, Tallaght, Dublin 24. Email: info@folens.ie

Poland: JUKA, ul. Renesansowa 38, Warsaw 01-905

Editor: Sara Peacock
Layout artist: Ken Vail Graphic Design, Cambridge
Illustrations: Celia Hart
Cover design: Ken Vail Graphic Design, Cambridge

First published 2006 by Folens Limited.

Every effort has been made to contact copyright holders of material used in this publication. If any copyright holder has been overlooked, we should be pleased to make any necessary arrangements.

British Library Cataloguing in Publication Data. A catalogue record for this publication is available from the British Library.

ISBN 1-84303-860-9

# Contents

*Music Works*
## Creative Approach to Music in Education

Dear Teacher,

We hope you find this music resource pack helpful and easy to use. The main idea behind this pack is for your lesson-planning to be done for you to enable you to relax. No special musical ability or aptitude is required!

### What does *Music Works* do?

*Music Works* provides three sections for every age group. Within each pack are different themes, for example, for Years 3 and 4, Friendship, Bullying and World music.

Each individual pack contains six 40-minute lesson plans (along with a CD), all working towards the end performance of a specially composed and themed song. The emphasis is on learning through singing, but percussion and rap is also used and, along the way, many music curriculum requirements for Key Stages 1 and 2 will be met.

You are led through each step simply, using the CD tracks to guide you through the song, vocal exercises, rhythm and pulse exercises (all of which are very easy to follow).

Each pack may also be used cross-curriculum with English.

### What's different about *Music Works*? The 'WOW' Factor!

This pack has an original contemporary 'pop' song, written especially for *Music Works*. This means the children are more likely to want to engage with it as they will like the sound of it!

Each song has space for a rap in it. Part of this is already written and part of it needs to be written by the class. This seems to work especially well with some of the boys – they identify with rap more easily than some other forms of music and think it's 'cool' to join in with! It encourages them to express themselves and give ideas.

The children also feel the song becomes theirs and is part of their genre – not the teacher's.

### How to get the best out of *Music Works*

Read through the lesson plan and get comfortable with starting and stopping your CD player so you don't spend time during the lesson trying to figure out how it works. All machines are slightly different and can thwart the best of us! Make sure you have a good CD player that has sufficient volume.

The feeling that the children 'own' the song rather than the teacher is key to the success and enjoyment of *Music Works* and should be encouraged. (For example, I might say, 'Well, you could do that rap movement with your hands', which I imitate badly and say, 'Oh I can't do it, I'm too old, you show me.' I let them laugh at my pitiful attempts to try to move and rap and they will try to show me and the other children how to do it.)

### Children with differing abilities

Children who may not engage in other subjects well can be very musical and the difference between learners is far less obvious.

Ensure that less able children make a big contribution to the rap section. A sense of ownership starts to develop and the resultant building in their confidence is very rewarding.

**Note from the authors:**
We hope these lessons will be useful to you as a teacher and make learning about music fun for the children. Don't hesitate to let us know how things work or don't work for you so we can update our design and provide you with further resources for the future.

## Lesson 1 The song: 'Friendship'

## Music objective

Introducing the song and learning to sing part of it.

## Learning activity

◆ Doing a full vocal warm-up (QCA units 8:1 and 8:5).
◆ Learning basic techniques for building confidence in using the singing voice (QCA unit 8:1).
◆ Following and learning the verses and chorus of a new song (QCA units 8:4, 8:6 and 8:7).

## Learning activity

### Unit 8 Ongoing skills

*'This unit focuses on the development of the singing voice and other essential musical skills (listening skills, aural memory and physical skills) that should be a regular part of classroom work week-by-week.'*
*'Singing songs with control and using the voice expressively.'*
Children should learn:

◆ Section 1 – to develop their singing voices.
◆ Section 4 – to develop awareness of simple structures (phrases).
◆ Section 5 – to recognise changes in, and control, pitch.
◆ Section 6 – about how to express the meaning of songs.

*'Listening, memory and movement.'*

◆ Section 7 – Children should learn to listen with attention to detail and develop aural memory.

### Scottish attainment targets

*Using materials, techniques, skills and media (voice)*

◆ Level A – Show ability to memorise simple songs containing repetitive melodic and rhythmic patterns.
◆ Level B – Control rhythm, speed and leaps in melody.

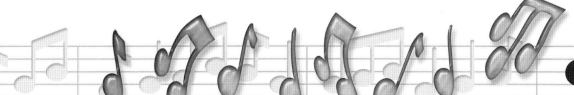

## Lesson 1 *The song:* 'Friendship'

**1** 🔘 Play TRACK 1 on the CD – 'Friendship'.

**2** Listen again, pointing out the structure of verse 1, verse 2, chorus, rap, chorus, percussion break and gap for own rap, and chorus. Explain to the children that there is space for their very own rap. Briefly talk in general about the theme of friendship – this is the theme of the song and the theme of the rap they will be writing.

**3** Vocal warm-up – we sing using our whole body, not just the vocal chords! We therefore need to make sure we are relaxed and open physically in order to release the voice. Take ten minutes to do the warm-up.

- ◆ Ask the children to stand in a circle and make sure they are standing in 'neutral' – with un-folded arms and legs shoulder-width apart. Ask them to imagine that their head is attached to a piece of string from above, which is pulling their head and shoulders up straight.

- ◆ Loosen up the body in whatever way is preferred (for example, rotating the head in a circle, doing large circles clockwise and anti-clockwise with the arms from the shoulder, circles with the hips, circles with the feet and knees, then shaking the whole leg away).

- ◆ Take deep breaths in from the abdomen (not the upper chest) to the count of four through the nose. Then breathe out slowly to the count of 20. (Ask the children to put their hands on their stomach so that they can feel it rising and falling as they breathe. This ensures diaphragmatic, rather than shallow breaths.)

- ◆ Repeat, now doing a 'Sss' sound on the out-breath (like a snake!).

- ◆ Repeat doing a 'Zzzzz' sound on the out-breath (like a bee).

- ◆ Repeat doing a hum on the out-breath.

- ◆ Take deep breaths in and do loud exaggerated sighs out, going from a high to a low noise.

- ◆ Have the children pretend they are chewing an extremely large toffee, making exaggerated chewing shapes with the mouth (this releases the jaw). Then ask them to open the mouth as wide as possible. Explain that, when we sing, we need to let the sound out and so need to exaggerate our words, opening our mouths wider than in speech.

## Lesson 1 The song: 'Friendship'

**4** Listen and follow TRACK 3 on the CD. The CD guides you through this voice-releasing exercise in the form of 'call and answer'. (Something is shouted on the CD, there is a gap for you and the children to copy this and shout it back. Come in after the count of four.) The children should push their elbows back in one short movement and, at the same time, release a very loud 'Hey' sound. Point out that normally teachers want children to be quiet, but now you want them to be as loud as they can be.

**5** Listen and follow TRACK 4 on the CD. This is the chorus of the song, repeated a few times. Sing along and learn the words.

**6** Listen and follow TRACK 5 on the CD. These are the two verses of the song repeated. Sing along and learn the words.

**7** Play through TRACK 1 again with the children singing along with what they have learned.

## Chill out time!

Have the children sit down at their desks. Each child should lay their head on their arms with eyes closed, breathing slowly through their nose. Ask them to listen to the sounds around them in silence. After one minute, ask them to put up their hands and say what they've heard.

# Lesson 2 ) Rhythm

*Note – You will be using the percussion trolley for this lesson.*

## Music objective

Learning about rhythm and pulse.

## Learning activity

- ◆ Playing percussion (rhythm and pulse) for the percussion break in the song (QCA unit 10:1).
- ◆ Doing a vocal warm-up (QCA units 8:1 and 8:5).
- ◆ Remembering the chorus and verses of the song (QCA units 8:4, 8:6 and 8:7).
- ◆ Recapping basic techniques for building confidence in using the singing voice (QCA unit 8:1).

## Learning activity

### Unit 8 Ongoing skills

*'This unit focuses on the development of the singing voice and other essential musical skills (listening skills, aural memory and physical skills) that should be a regular part of classroom work week-by-week.'*
*'Singing songs with control and using the voice expressively.'*
Children should learn:

- ◆ Section 1 – to develop their singing voices.
- ◆ Section 4 – to develop awareness of simple structures (phrases).
- ◆ Section 5 – to recognise changes in, and control, pitch.
- ◆ Section 6 – about how to express the meaning of songs.

*'Listening, memory and movement.'*

- ◆ Section 7 – Children should learn to listen with attention to detail and develop aural memory.

### Unit 10 Exploring rhythmic patterns

*'In this unit, children extend their understanding of rhythmic patterns, and in particular, ostinato. They create their own patterns and play them separately and in combination with other patterns. They identify repeated patterns in different types of music.'*

- ◆ Section 1 – Children should learn about repeated rhythmic patterns.

###  Scottish attainment targets

*Using materials, techniques, skills and media (instruments)*

- ◆ Level A – Use basic playing techniques such as shaking and tapping, keeping the beat and repeating simply rhythmic patterns.
- ◆ Level B – Play simple rhythmic parts, showing some control over speed and volume in response to simple signals of direction.

## Lesson 2 ) *Rhythm*

**1**  Play TRACK 1 on the CD – 'Friendship'. Ask the children to sing along quietly with what they learned in the previous lesson.

**2** Listen to TRACK 6 on the CD. This plays the pulse of the song. Clap along, counting out loud 1, 2, 3 and 4. Tell the children that the pulse always has a steady regular beat.

**3** Listen to the rhythm on TRACK 7 on the CD. Explain that rhythm is different from pulse – the beats aren't evenly spaced. Encourage the children to clap the rhythm.

**4** Split the class into two groups – ask one half to clap the steady pulse, and the other to clap the rhythm on top.

**5** See if the children can come up with another rhythm that fits with the pulse – this should be different from the old rhythm. If the children are having real difficulty with this, then listen to TRACK 8 on the CD, which has a second rhythm to learn.

**6** Split the class into three groups. Ask the first group to play the pulse, the second the first rhythm, and the third group the second rhythm. Add the groups one at a time so each group becomes established before the next is added.

**7** Hand out percussion instruments and distribute according to resources or preferences: for example, tambourines could play the pulse, woodblocks rhythm 1, and drums rhythm 2.

**8** 💿 Now, encourage the children to play along with TRACK 1 on the CD with their percussion instruments in the three groups.

**9** The children will sing again now, so do a short version of the vocal warm-up as outlined in Lesson 1.

**10** 💿 Ask the children to play and sing along to TRACK 1 without the percussion. Make sure voices are loud and clear. (They can try with percussion as well if there is time.)

**11** 💿 Play TRACK 2 (the backing track) to see if the children can sing up to the rap section, stopping there. It's only half-way through, but they will get used to *not* hearing the supporting voice on the CD.

**12** If any children would like, they could have the opportunity to sing the first or second verse solo, with the whole class joining in on the first chorus. Try to give a number of different children the chance to sing solo (they could stay in position rather than stand up in front of the class, if they prefer).

**Chill out time!**

Have the children sit down at their desks. Each child should lay their head on their arms with eyes closed, breathing slowly through their nose. Ask them to listen to the sounds around them in silence. After one minute, ask them to put up their hands and say what they've heard.

## Lesson 3 *Singing techniques*

## Music objective

Learning the rap section of the song and improving the quality of singing.

## Learning activity

◆ Singing a full vocal warm-up (QCA units 8:1 and 8:5).

◆ Stretching the voice further (QCA unit 8:1).

◆ Recapping on the verses and chorus of the song (QCA units 8:4, 8:6 and 8:7).

◆ Learning the 'rap' section of the song (QCA units 8:4 and 8:7).

## Learning activity

### Unit 8 Ongoing skills

'This unit focuses on the development of the singing voice and other essential musical skills (listening skills, aural memory and physical skills) that should be a regular part of classroom work week-by-week.'
'Singing songs with control and using the voice expressively.'
Children should learn:

◆ Section 1 – to develop their singing voices.

◆ Section 4 – to develop awareness of simple structures (phrases).

◆ Section 5 – to recognise changes in, and control, pitch.

◆ Section 6 – about how to express the meaning of songs.

'Listening, memory and movement.'

◆ Section 7 – Children should learn to listen with attention to detail and develop aural memory.

### Scottish attainment targets

*Using materials, techniques, skills and media (voice)*

◆ Level B – Show a greater ability to sing in tune with others; control rhythm, speed and leaps in melody.

**1** Do the full vocal warm-up as outlined in Lesson 1. Take no more than ten minutes.

**2** Listen to TRACK 9 on the CD. This is part of a more advanced warm-up. Tell the children that they are going to stretch their vocal range both higher and lower. TRACK 9 is a 'call and answer' melody for them to copy. The CD does the call and the children can sing along with the answer. You can use 'Hello, lo, low' to reach the lower notes. It may be too low for them to sing but encourage them to have fun trying. Encourage the children to feel how the note travels down the body as they sing lower.

**3** Listen to TRACK 10 on the CD. This track has a 'call and answer' melody for the children to copy. The voice on the CD sings the call and the children can sing along with the answer. Try to use a melody to reach the higher notes. Ask the children if they can feel how the note travels up the body, as they sing higher and higher.

**4** Listen to TRACK 12 on the CD. This takes the children up through the whole vocal range. This is 'sing along' not 'call and answer'. Tell the children that the higher they go, the wider they must open their mouths and think 'up and back'.

**5** Listen again to TRACK 1 on the CD. Ask the children, as a class, to sing along at full volume with the verses and chorus that have been learned. Your class should be in fine voice now after the full warm-up. Encourage them to be aware of where they are singing from in their body. Tell them that the high notes will resonate in their head, the middle ones in their chest and the lower ones in their abdomen. Ask if the high notes feel easier to sing after doing the extended warm-up.

# Lesson 3 *Singing techniques*

**6** Let TRACK 1 play on to the rap section and tell the children to listen carefully.

**7** With the class, listen and sing along to TRACK 11 (the rap section) so that the children can learn it.

**8** Replay TRACK 1 for the class. They can now sing along to the whole thing, leaving a gap for the percussion break and extra rap section, which will be added later.

**9** Play TRACK 2 (the backing track) and see if the children can sing the song all the way through. Leave the rap for now. Ask the children if anyone would like to stand *in front* of the class and sing a verse solo. Perhaps some would like to do it in small groups of two or three pupils.

## Chill out time!

Have the children sit down at their desks. Each child should lay their head on their arms with eyes closed, breathing slowly through their nose. Ask them to listen to the sounds around them in silence. Can they feel their heart beat? Their breathing? Their stomach rumbling? After one minute, ask them to put up their hands and say what they've heard and felt.

13

# Lesson 4  The rap

## Music objective

Writing their own rap for the rap section on the theme of friendship.
Creating rhythmic verse, matching words with metre.

## Learning activity

◆ Creating a series of (possibly) rhyming phrases that fits with the pulse of the song, so creating a rap (QCA unit 10:4).

◆ Practising this rap along with the relevant backing section of the song (QCA units 8:4 and 8:7).

## Learning activity

### Unit 8 Ongoing skills

*'This unit focuses on the development of the singing voice and other essential musical skills (listening skills, aural memory and physical skills) that should be a regular part of classroom work week-by-week.'*
*'Singing songs with control and using the voice expressively.'*

◆ Section 4 – Children should learn to develop awareness of simple structures (phrases).

*'Listening, memory and movement.'*

◆ Section 7 – Children should learn to listen with attention to detail and develop aural memory.

### Unit 10 Exploring rhythmic patterns

*'In this unit, children extend their understanding of rhythmic patterns, and in particular, ostinato. They create their own patterns and play them separately and in combination with other patterns. They identify repeated patterns in different types of music.'*

◆ Section 4 – Children should learn to compose music using rhythmic ostinati based on spoken phrase.

 **Scottish attainment targets**

*Expressing feelings, ideas, thought and solutions (creating and designing)*

◆ Level A – Select appropriate sound sources and combine and link sounds to convey effect in a short invention.

◆ Level B – Create simple sound pictures, conveying an imaginative response to a stimulus.

# Friendship
## Lesson 4 — *The rap*

**1** 🎵 Play the song on TRACK 1 and ask the children to clap to the pulse. If they can't remember, demonstrate to them how to do this.

**2** 🎵 Listen to the rap section of the CD (TRACK 11).

**3** Discussion time! Ask the children to come up with their thoughts and feelings about friendship. Tell them to think of good and bad times, what makes a good friend and when they have been a good friend. Write all these down on the whiteboard. These can be just words and phrases, or fully formed sentences.

**4** Put the children into groups and ask them to decide between them what they definitely want to include in their rap. When the groups feed back to the whole class, circle or star their choices on the board.

**5** Encourage the children to clap along to the rhythm of the words of the existing rap. Using this rhythm, try to fit in some of the 'friendship' phrases they have chosen. You may have to adapt them – lengthen them or shorten them for example – to fit with the pulse. Ask the children to think of relevant words that rhyme with some of the phrases that you have chosen. Arrange them in a fitting order. (Note – the rap doesn't have to rhyme – it only has to make sense!)

**6** There is a gap for the rap in the track. Tell the children that after the second time they hear:

> *Friendship, all we need*
> *Friendship, all we need*
> *Give a little love and take a little love, now*
> *Friendship, all we need, sing.*
> *Friendship, all we need*
> *Friendship, all we need*

they should come in with their new rap, keeping to the pulse. Ask the children if it fits, or if it is too long or short, then encourage them to cut it down or add to it as required.

**7** Practise your rap! (Have the children clap along with the pulse to help them to rap in time.)

**8** Play TRACK 2 and have the children try to sing all the way to the rap, then add in the rap section. Ask the children who they think are the coolest rappers and to choose five or six children to perform the rap. Explain that it's good to vary the texture by having a smaller group perform the rap and then everybody coming in together smartly on the next section.

### Chill out time!

Have the children sit down at their desks. Each child should lay their head on their arms with eyes closed, breathing slowly through their nose. Ask them to think about times when they were a really good friend to someone – it doesn't have to be someone their own age, it could be an adult or a family member. Ask them to think about how it felt to do something good for someone. Did it make them feel proud? Happy? Is there someone they could be a better friend to at the moment?

**Lesson 5** *Moods and feelings*

*Note – You will need the percussion trolley (tuned and un-tuned instruments), recorders and any other instruments available for this lesson.*

## Music objective

Identifying different moods with different pieces of music; improvising musical moods; recapping the song.

## Learning activity

◆ Listening to three contrasting pieces of music and identifying which animal they portray (QCA unit 9:1).

◆ Recapping basic techniques for building confidence in using the singing voice (QCA unit 8:1).

## Learning activity

### Unit 8 Ongoing skills

*'This unit focuses on the development of the singing voice and other essential musical skills (listening skills, aural memory and physical skills) that should be a regular part of classroom work week-by-week.'*
*'Singing songs with control and using the voice expressively.'*
◆ Section 1 – Children should learn to develop their singing voices.

### Unit 9 Animal magic – Exploring descriptive sounds

*'In this unit, children learn to recognise how sounds can be used to describe different things, e.g. animals. Using this understanding, they create their own music in pairs, add movement and narration and rehearse towards a final performance for others. During the unit they explore how the elements of pitch, duration, dynamics and tempo can be combined to describe different sounds, e.g. animal sounds.'*
*'Introduction: how can music describe different animals?'*
◆ Section 1 – Children should learn to identify how music can be used descriptively, for example to represent different animal characteristics.

### Scottish attainment targets
*Evaluating and appreciating*
◆ Levels A–C – Observe, listen, reflect on, describe and respond to musical sounds in the environment and, in Level C, give opinions of music and accept the opinions of others.
◆ Level B – Discuss the characteristics of music with a clearly identifiable mood in terms of speed or volume.

1　 Listen to TRACKS 13, 14 and 15 with the class. Encourage the children to think of three animals – a bird, a lion and a shark – and ask them to identify which piece of music best describes which animal. Ask them the following questions:

- ◆ Why did the pieces of music sound different?

- ◆ What instrument or sound made the shark sound dangerous?

- ◆ What instrument or sound made the lion powerful?

- ◆ What instrument or sound made the bird gentle?

Listen to each track again and encourage the children to try to identify these things. (Note: there's no right or wrong answer here, just different feelings.)

2　Split the class into three groups and ask each group to choose an animal. (Note: it may be easier to assign a contrasting animal to each group such as a horse, a butterfly and an elephant) Allow the children to pick instruments from the trolley and then ask each group to create a short piece describing their animal using tuned and un-tuned instruments. Have the children think about what instruments might be useful to help describe the feel of their animal. For example, a horse could be suggested by rhythmic clops, a butterfly by gentle tinkling sounds, shakers and so on, and an elephant by deep, loud, slow, long-held recorder notes.

3　Carry out a short vocal warm-up. You could ask the children how to do this first to see how they are learning and reminding them to relax themselves in order to start singing.

## Lesson 5 Moods and feelings

**4** 🔘 Practise all the children have learned so far by singing and rapping along to TRACK 2, which is the backing track. After the second chorus, there are ten bars for a percussion break. Using their instruments, the children can play here the rhythms they practised in lesson 2. They will need to be ready to begin the rap again straight afterwards.

**5** Ask the children how they think it is going. Are they improving each time? Are they enunciating the words properly so an audience can understand what they are singing?

**6** Practise the song again, correcting the mistakes made. See if the children can identify any improvements that can be made.

**7** Divide the class in two and have one half stand up and perform the song to the rest of the class. The half that are watching are allowed to pull faces at the performers in an attempt to disrupt them and put them off their singing. They're not allowed to make a sound, though! Change over and repeat the process with the other half of the class performing.

### Chill out time!

Have the children sit down at their desks. Each child should lay their head on their arms with eyes closed, breathing slowly through their nose. Ask them to think about their favourite animal. What type of music would fit with their animal? If they could pick any instrument, which one would they choose to play its music? Encourage them to try to imagine a film in their head of the animal in its natural habitat, moving to music that they are composing.

**Friendship**

**Lesson 6** *The final rehearsal and performance*

*Note – You will be using the percussion trolley for this lesson.*

## Music objective

Practising performance skills and final polishing of the song.

## Learning activity

◆ Full vocal warm-up (QCA units 8:1 and 8:5).

◆ Practising the song (QCA unit 8:7).

## Learning activity

### Unit 8 Ongoing skills

*'This unit focuses on the development of the singing voice and other essential musical skills (listening skills, aural memory and physical skills) that should be a regular part of classroom work week-by-week.'*

*'Singing songs with control and using the voice expressively.'*

Children should learn:

◆ Section 1 – to develop their singing voices.

◆ Section 5 – to recognise changes in, and control, pitch.

*'Listening, memory and movement.'*

◆ Section 7 – Children should learn to listen with attention to detail and develop aural memory.

### Scottish attainment targets

*Expressing feelings, ideas, thought and solutions*

◆ Levels A–E – Invent music individually and in groups, displaying initiative and using knowledge of sound and structures gained in their explorations.

*Evaluating and appreciating*

◆ Level C – Give opinions of own music making and that of others and accept and offer suggestions for improvement.

## Lesson 6   *The final rehearsal and performance*

**1**  💿 As before, take the class through a warm-up and an advanced warm-up. Use TRACKS 9, 10 and 12 on the CD.

**2**  Ask the children to sit down in two separate groups. (This could be done with girls being in one group and boys in another.)

**3**  💿 Play TRACK 1 and tell the children to sing quietly through the song. This is to remind everyone of the musical format.

**4**  Explain to the children that they are going to practise performing and stress the importance of singing with good diction and clarity so that the audience can really understand the words. Tell them that it is necessary to exaggerate the shapes of the words with the mouth while singing – it is not enough to sing words as we would speak them. Explain that it may feel strange to exaggerate the word shapes, but to the audience they will seem just right! Ask the class as a whole to speak through the song, practising the exaggerated word shapes. (This may raise a laugh or two!)

**5**  Next, ask Group A to perform to Group B. Tell the performing group to smile, look at the audience, stand up straight and sing the words with good diction! Remember to get percussion instruments ready too.

**6**  Encourage Group B to give feedback to Group A. Ask the children to put their hands up with their comments about the performance. You can help by asking them to comment about specific areas, for example:

◆ Do people know the words?

◆ Are they enunciating them properly so we can understand them?

◆ Was the singing loud enough?

◆ Did the percussion break happen as planned?

◆ Did the rappers come in at the right place?

◆ How could it be improved?

◆ What went well and sounded good?

**Lesson 6** *The final rehearsal and performance*

**7** Now swap the groups over and repeat the process, so Group B performs to Group A. Group A should give feedback as before. Encourage them to think of some new comments or observations.

**8** If necessary, now would be a good time to practise any individual section that needs some extra work, before having the whole group play along to TRACK 2 again.

**9** Practise the performance over TRACK 2 with all the children together. (You might like to add movement at this point. For example, when it gets to the rap parts, ask those not rapping to bob down on one knee and jump up as soon as their part comes back in.) Have the whole class perform to you, making sure they are standing up straight, looking out to the 'audience', singing and enunciating loud and clear (without shouting).

**Chill out time!**

Have the children sit down at their desks. Each child should lay their head on their arms with eyes closed, breathing slowly through their nose. Ask them to listen to the sounds around them in silence. After one minute, ask them to put up their hands and say what they've heard.

# Friendship

**Verse 1**   You and I may disagree
Someone else comes in between
Right to the end
We'll be friends.

**Verse 2**   If you should find a friend that's true,
Someone who'll be good to you,
We all depend on our
Good friends.

**Chorus**   Let's stay friends,
Let's stay friends,
Right to the end
We'll be friends.

Let's stay friends,
Let's stay friends,
Right to the end
We'll be friends.

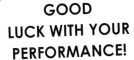

**GOOD LUCK WITH YOUR PERFORMANCE!**
*(Note: This performance can take place in the classroom, in front of the whole school at assembly, or as part of a school play. Wherever you perform it, make sure you all have fun doing it!)*

**Rap**   Friendship, all we need
Friendship, all we need
Give a little love and take a little love, now
Friendship, all we need, sing
Friendship, all we need
Friendship, all we need
In the playground on your own
Watching everybody else have fun.
Feeling that you're so alone,
But remember it won't last long.
Remember – listen to this song.

**Chorus**   Let's stay friends,
Let's stay friends,
Right to the end
We'll be friends.

**New rap**

**Chorus**   Let's stay friends,
Let's stay friends,
Right to the end
We'll be friends.

## Lesson 1  *The song:* 'Bully'

### Music objective

Introducing the song and learning to sing part of it.

### Learning activity

◆ Doing a full vocal warm-up (QCA units 8:1 and 8:5).

◆ Learning basic techniques for building confidence in using the singing voice (QCA unit 8:1).

◆ Following and learning the verses and chorus of a new song (QCA units 8:4, 8:6 and 8:7).

### Learning activity

**Unit 8 Ongoing skills**

*'This unit focuses on the development of the singing voice and other essential musical skills (listening skills, aural memory and physical skills) that should be a regular part of classroom work week-by-week.'*
*'Singing songs with control and using the voice expressively.'*
Children should learn:

◆ Section 1 – to develop their singing voices.

◆ Section 4 – to develop awareness of simple structures (phrases).

◆ Section 5 – to recognise changes in, and control, pitch.

◆ Section 6 – about how to express the meaning of songs.

*'Listening, memory and movement.'*

◆ Section 7 – Children should learn to listen with attention to detail and develop aural memory.

### Scottish attainment targets

*Using materials, techniques, skills and media (voice)*

◆ Level A – Show ability to memorise simple songs containing repetitive melodic and rhythmic patterns.

◆ Level B – Control rhythm, speed and leaps in melody.

## Lesson 1  The song: 'Bully'

**1** 🔘 Play TRACK 16 on the CD – 'Bully' – and ask the children to listen carefully.

**2** Listen again, pointing out the structure of verse 1, verse 2, percussion break, rap, gap for the children's rap, then the last verse. Explain to the children that there is space for their very own rap. Briefly talk in general about the theme of the song and of the rap the children will be writing – bullying.

**3** Prepare the class with a vocal warm-up. We sing using our whole body, not just the vocal chords! We therefore need to make sure we are relaxed and open physically in order to release the voice. Take ten minutes to do the warm-up.

◆ Ask the children to stand in a circle and make sure they are standing in 'neutral' – with unfolded arms and legs shoulder-width apart. Ask them to imagine that their head is attached to a piece of string from above, which is pulling their head and shoulders up straight.

◆ Loosen up the body in whatever way is preferred (for example, rotating the head in a circle, doing large circles clockwise and anti-clockwise with the arms from the shoulder, circles with the hips, circles with the feet and knees, then shaking the whole leg away).

◆ Take a deep breath into the lower abdomen to the count of three through the nose, then continue to breathe in for a further three counts, bringing the breath into the upper chest. Then breathe out slowly to a count of 20. This ensures diaphragmatic, rather than shallow, breaths. (Ask the children to put one hand on their stomach and the other on their upper chest, so they can feel them both rising and falling as they breathe.)

◆ Repeat, now doing a 'Sss' sound on the out-breath.

◆ Repeat doing a hum on the out-breath.

◆ Take deep breaths in and do loud exaggerated yawns going from a high to a low noise. Ask the children if they can feel the note go from high to low in their body as well.

**4** The diaphragm. Explain to the children that the diaphragm is a strange-shaped muscle that can be felt if we put our hands just below the rib cage and say a short, sharp 'Cah'. Tell them to do this several times and to see if they can feel their diaphragm moving – they will need to push quite hard from the tummy. Next, ask them to try the same thing, but with their hands on their backs, just above the kidneys, to see if they can feel the diaphragm moving there too. Tell them that, when we sing, we use this muscle as our 'volume pedal' to push the sound out: the harder we push with our diaphragm, the louder the sound. To exercise the diaphragm go through the alphabet (consonants only) to the rhythm of 'Ba, Ba, Ba, Barbaran' (as in the Beach Boys song!), so: 'ba, ba, ba, ba-ba-ba, ba' then 'ca, ca, ca, ca-ca-ca ca', and so on. Whilst they do this, they should keep their hands resting on their belly-button area so they can feel how hard their diaphragm is working.

**5** Listen and follow TRACK 18 on the CD, which guides you through a voice-stretching exercise. Something is sung on the CD, and then there is a gap for the children to copy this and sing it back. It may be sung high or low, loud or soft, so encourage the children to be aware of all these things and try to copy them when they sing the response.

**6** Listen and follow TRACK 19 on the CD. This is the first verse of the song. Sing along as a class and learn it.

**7** Listen and follow TRACK 20 on the CD. These are the second and third verses of the song. Sing along and learn them.

**8** Play through TRACK 16 again with the children singing along with what they have learned.

## Chill out time!

Have the children sit down at their desks. Each child should lay their head on their arms with eyes closed, breathing slowly through their nose. Ask them to check how their bodies are feeling after all that singing. Do they feel more tired or livelier? Are their stomachs hurting from using their diaphragms so much? Do they feel more relaxed, or happier, or just the same? Sit for a minute in silence and calm and then ask for the children to put their hands up if they have any feelings to share.

# Lesson 2 Rhythm

Note – You will need a reggae track of your choice to play (for example, any Bob Marley or UB40 song). You will need the percussion trolley for this lesson.

## Music objective

Learning about rhythm and pulse.

## Learning activity

◆ Playing percussion (rhythm and pulse) for the percussion break in the song (QCA unit 10:1).

◆ Doing a vocal warm-up (QCA units 8:1 and 8:5).

## Learning activity

### Unit 8 Ongoing skills

*'This unit focuses on the development of the singing voice and other essential musical skills (listening skills, aural memory and physical skills) that should be a regular part of classroom work week-by-week.'*
*'Singing songs with control and using the voice expressively.'*
Children should learn:

◆ Section 1 – to develop their singing voices.

◆ Section 5 – to recognise changes in, and control, pitch.

### Unit 10 Exploring rhythmic patterns

*'In this unit, children extend their understanding of rhythmic patterns, and in particular, ostinato. They create their own patterns and play them separately and in combination with other patterns. They identify repeated patterns in different types of music.'*

◆ Section 1 – Children should learn about repeated rhythmic patterns.

### Scottish attainment targets

*Using materials, techniques, skills and media (instruments)*

◆ Level A – Use basic playing techniques such as shaking and tapping, keeping the beat and repeating simply rhythmic patterns.

◆ Level B – Play simple rhythmic parts, showing some control over speed and volume in response to simple signals of direction.

##  Bullying

## Lesson 2 Rhythm

**1** 🎵 Play TRACK 16 on the CD – 'Bully'. Ask the children to sing quietly along with what they learned in the previous lesson.

**2** 🎵 Listen to TRACK 21 on the CD. This plays the pulse of the song. Clap along with the children, counting out loud 1, 2, 3 and 4. Explain that pulse always has a steady regular beat.

**3** 🎵 Listen to the rhythm on TRACK 22 on the CD. Explain that rhythm is different to pulse – the beats aren't evenly spaced. Clap the rhythm and point out that it is a 'reggae' rhythm. (Note: You could have a brief chat/ explanation about reggae here, if you wish.)

**4** Split the class into two groups – one half should clap the reggae rhythm, then the other should clap the same reggae rhythm back, like a call and response.

**5** Now split the class into three groups, asking the first to clap the 'call' part of the reggae rhythm, the second group the 'response' to the reggae rhythm and the third the pulse of the song. Add the groups one at a time so each group becomes established before the next is added.

**6** Hand out percussion instruments and distribute according to resources or preferences – for example, woodblocks for those children playing the pulse, drums for rhythm 1 and tambourines for rhythm 2.

**7** 🎵 Next, ask the children to play along with TRACK 16 on the CD with their percussion instruments using the three groups. They can sing along quietly and then come in on the percussion break after the second chorus. Was the percussion in time? (Note: If it is too hard for the children to all come in together, then bring groups in one at a time as was done earlier. There are eight bars for the percussion to happen in, so plenty of time to stagger the entries in three stages.)

28

**8** The children will now be singing properly again, so do a short version of the vocal warm-up as outlined in Lesson 1, picking the bits you feel the children need.

**9** 💿 Sing along to TRACK 16, this time making sure voices are loud and clear. Ask the children to come in with the percussion after the second chorus.

**10** How did it go? Ask the children to suggest what went right and what went wrong. Was the singing loud enough? Was the percussion in time? What needs to happen next time they practise to make it even better?

## Chill out time!

Have the children sit down at their desks. Each child should lay their head on their arms with eyes closed, breathing slowly through their nose. Play the reggae track that you have brought with you and ask them to listen to the rhythm and to see if they can hear how the rhythm is similar to the one they have just performed. Once the track is finished, ask for volunteers to try to say (or demonstrate) how it is similar and how it is different. Is it faster? Is it slower?

# Lesson 3 The rap and pentatonic scales

*Note – You will need a piano or a keyboard for this lesson.*

## Music objective

Learning the rap section of the song and learning the pentatonic scale.

## Learning activity

◆ Learning the pentatonic scale (QCA unit 12:1).

◆ Learning the 'rap' section of the song (QCA units 8:4 and 8:7).

◆ Recapping on the verses and chorus of the song (QCA units 8:4, 8:6 and 8:7).

## Learning activity

### Unit 8 Ongoing skills

*'This unit focuses on the development of the singing voice and other essential musical skills (listening skills, aural memory and physical skills) that should be a regular part of classroom work week-by-week.'*
*'Singing songs with control and using the voice expressively.'*
Children should learn:

◆ Section 4 – to develop awareness of simple structures (phrases).

◆ Section 6 – about how to express the meaning of songs.

*'Listening, memory and movement.'*

◆ Section 7 – Children should learn to listen with attention to detail and develop aural memory.

### Unit 12 Dragon scales – exploring pentatonic scales

*'This unit develops children's ability to recognise, and use, pentatonic scales and create short melodies and accompaniments.'*

◆ Section 1 – Children should learn about pentatonic scales and how they are used in music.

### Scottish attainment targets

*Using materials, techniques, skills and media (voice)*

◆ Level B – Show a greater ability to sing in tune with others; control rhythm, speed and leaps in melody.

◆ Level C – Sing together confidently in unison.

**Lesson 3** *The rap and pentatonic scales*

**1** Ask the children to gather round the piano or keyboard. Start to play the black notes from about halfway up, starting from the first one of the group of three (F#). Slowly play up for the next five black notes (i.e. the set of three then the next set of two). This is a pentatonic scale (F#, G#, A#, C#, D#). Pent means five, as in pentagon or pentacle. This scale has just five notes in it and then starts again exactly the same, but higher up. Ordinary scales have seven notes in them, so the pentatonic scale has a special sound because it uses only five. We miss out steps four and seven of an ordinary scale. Show how we can see the missing steps on the keyboard or piano: steps 1, 2 and 3 are there in the black notes, and then we have a jump to the next set of two black notes, then another jump to the next set of three to start the scale again.

**2** Let some of the children take turns in having a go on the keyboard or piano. They can change the order of the notes to make a tune out of the pentatonic scale, as long as they just stick to the black notes.

**3** Listen to TRACK 27 on the CD. This is an example of an ordinary scale, followed by a pentatonic scale.

**4** Now listen to TRACKS 28 and 29 on the CD. They are two examples of tunes made from pentatonic scales. Encourage the children to listen out for the pentatonic scale's special sound. Traditional Chinese and Japanese music is written using this scale, as is a lot of Scottish and Irish music.

**5** Listen to TRACK 30. This is actually the tune for the chorus of 'Bully', but it is also written on the pentatonic scale – ask which of the children can hear this.

**6** Do a shortened vocal warm-up as outlined in Lesson 1. Choose the activities you feel the children benefit from the most.

**7** Sing along quietly to the verses and choruses of TRACK 16 and have a good listen to the rap section. (Note: When the rap goes into the four-line section 'BULLY – stop pulling her hair', you could split the class into two groups and have one half doing the call – 'BULLY' and the other half doing the answer 'Stop pulling her hair'.)

## Lesson 3 ) The rap and pentatonic scales

**8** Listen, learn and then rap along to TRACK 26, which is the rap section on its own. This will take several practices for the children to master.

**9** Return to TRACK 16 – the children can now sing along to the whole thing, leaving a gap for the percussion break and the extra rap section they will be writing. Tell them to remember that they are singing the notes of the pentatonic scale in the choruses. (Note: If you have time, the children could practise the percussion break at this point as well, clapping their rhythms.)

### Chill out time!

Have the children sit down at their desks. Each child should lay their head on their arms with eyes closed, breathing slowly through their nose. Ask them to imagine the song 'Bully' playing quietly in their heads and encourage them to think about the words and what they mean to them. Explain that, in the next lesson, they will be writing some of their own words to add to the song so ask them to consider what sort of thing they would like to say about bullying. They could put their hands up to volunteer their thoughts, but keep it short! Do take notes on anything that may be useful for the next lesson's lyric-writing session.

## Lesson 4 ) *The rap*

## *Music objective*

Writing their own rap on the theme of bullying – that is, creating rhythmic verse to match words with metre.

## *Learning activity*

◆ Creating a series of (possibly) rhyming phrases that fits with the pulse of the song, so creating a rap (QCA unit 10:4).

◆ Practising this rap along with the relevant backing section of the song (QCA units 8:4 and 8:7).

## *Learning activity*

### Unit 8 Ongoing skills

*'This unit focuses on the development of the singing voice and other essential musical skills (listening skills, aural memory and physical skills) that should be a regular part of classroom work week-by-week.'*
*'Singing songs with control and using the voice expressively.'*

◆ Section 4 – Children should learn to develop awareness of simple structures (phrases).

 *'Listening, memory and movement.'*

◆ Section 7 – Children should learn to listen with attention to detail and develop aural memory.

### Unit 10 Play it again – exploring rhythmic patterns

*'This unit develops children's ability to create simple rhythmic patterns and perform them rhythmically using notation as a support.'*
*'Bringing it all together.'*

◆ Section 4 – Children should learn to compose music using rhythmic ostinati based on spoken phrase.

### Scottish attainment targets

*Expressing feelings, ideas, thought and solutions (creating and designing)*

◆ Level A – Select appropriate sound sources and combine and link sounds to convey effect in a short invention.

◆ Level B – Create simple sound pictures, conveying an imaginative response to a stimulus.

**1** Play the song 'Bully' (TRACK 16 on the CD) to the class and ask the children to clap the pulse.

**2** Listen to the rap section of the CD (TRACK 26).

**3** Discussion time! Have ready any notes that you took from the last session's 'Chill out time' to feed back to the children. Get the children to come up with their thoughts and feelings about bullying. (*Note: This is obviously a sensitive area and you need to make clear that children can come and talk privately to you or an appropriate adult if they need to. Do follow the guidelines laid out in the school's bullying policy.*) Have any of the children seen someone being bullied? What should they do if they witness someone being bullied? Have any of the children been bullied themselves? Have any of them actually bullied anyone themselves? Write all the children's ideas down on the whiteboard: these can be just words, phrases or fully formed sentences. (Note: This is a good opportunity to gently encourage anyone to speak who you feel may have suffered bullying or has bullied themselves.)

**4** Pick out as a team what you definitely want to include in your rap and circle these words or phrases on the whiteboard.

**5** Clap along to the rhythm of the words of the existing rap with the children. Use this rhythm to try to fit in some of the phrases you have chosen on bullying. You may have to adapt them – lengthen, shorten and so on to fit with the pulse. Ask the children to think of relevant words that rhyme with some of the phrases that you have chosen. Arrange them in a fitting order. (Note: if you're struggling, it may be easier to stick with the format of the original rap, adding your own phrase after the word 'BULLY'.)

# Lesson 4 · *The rap*

**6** There's a gap for the children's rap in the track after they hear 'BULLY – stop pulling her hair. BULLY – you're not being fair. BULLY – we're not impressed. BULLY – just give it a rest.' They should come in with their new rap, keeping to the pulse. Does it fit, or is it too long or short? Ask the children to cut it down or add to it as required.

**7** Practise the rap. (It will help the children rap in time if they clap the pulse.)

**8** If time allows, practise the rap in context, singing along quietly to TRACK 16. Encourage the children to say the rap loud and clear in the relevant gap.

**9** Play TRACK 16 and sing through the whole song and rap. Then play TRACK 17 to see if the children can sing it all again but without the voice on the CD to help them. Ask them to really shout out at the end, as if scolding or telling off the bully.

## Chill out time!

Have the children sit down at their desks. Each child should lay their head on their arms with eyes closed, breathing slowly through their nose. Get them to think about the feelings that people shared about bullying in the discussion time. Ask them to think about whether they have learned anything, if they would act differently now if they saw someone being bullied, or if they got picked on themselves. After a minute, get children to put their hands up if they have anything to say.

**Bullying**

## Lesson 5  *Moods and feelings*

*Note – You will need the percussion trolley (tuned and untuned), recorders and any other instruments available for this lesson.*

### Music objective

Identifying different moods with different pieces of music; improvising musical moods; recapping the song.

### Learning activity

◆ Listening to three contrasting pieces of music and identifying which emotions they portray (QCA unit 9:1).

◆ Recapping basic techniques for building confidence in using the singing voice (QCA unit 8:1).

◆ Remembering the chorus, rap and verses of the song (QCA unit 8:7).

### Learning activity

#### Unit 8 Ongoing skills

*'This unit focuses on the development of the singing voice and other essential musical skills (listening skills, aural memory and physical skills) that should be a regular part of classroom work week-by-week.'*

*'Singing songs with control and using the voice expressively.'*

Children should learn:

◆ Section 1 – to develop their singing voices.

*'Listening, memory and movement.'*

◆ Section 7 – Children should learn to listen with attention to detail and develop aural memory.

#### Unit 9 Animal magic – Exploring descriptive sounds

*'In this unit, children learn to recognise how sounds can be used to describe different things, for example animals.'*

*'Introduction: how can music describe different animals?'*

◆ Section 1 – Children should learn to identify how music can be used descriptively, for example to represent different animal characteristics.

 **Scottish attainment targets**

*Evaluating and appreciating*

◆ Levels A–C – Observe, listen, reflect on, describe and respond to musical sounds in the environment and, in Level C, give opinions of music and accept the opinions of others.

◆ Level B – Discuss the characteristics of music with a clearly identifiable mood in terms of speed or volume.

**Lesson 5** *Moods and feelings*

**1** 💿 Listen to TRACKS 23, 24 and 25.

**2** Tell the children that each of the pieces describes a different emotion: fear (a frightened mouse), anger (an angry lion) and calmness (a gentle elephant). Ask them to identify which piece of music best describes which emotion.

**3** Ask the children the following questions:
- ◆ Why did the pieces of music sound different?
- ◆ What instrument or sound made the mouse frightened?
- ◆ What instrument or sound made the lion angry?
- ◆ What instrument or sound made the elephant calm and gentle?

**4** Listen to each track again and try to identify these things. Are the notes played quickly or slowly? High or low? Does it change by speeding up or slowing down? Does it change by getting louder or softer?

**5** Split the class into three groups and give each group a slip of paper with an emotion written down on it. They should keep their emotion secret from the other two groups. You could use the three emotions described above. (Note: it will be easier to assign a contrasting feeling to each group, as in the examples below.) They can then pick (or be given, if easier!) instruments from the trolley and each group should create a short musical piece describing their emotion using tuned and un-tuned instruments. Ask them to think about what instruments might be useful to help describe their emotion, for example:
- ◆ Anger – low sounds; sounds building in frequency and tempo; low drums and shakers.
- ◆ Fear – tinkly, gentle shakers; high trembly recorder notes and chime bars; all played at a high frequency and speed.
- ◆ Calmness – deep, gentle, slow, long-held recorder notes; chime bars played slowly and to a steady pulse; unchanging speed and volume.

Note: They could even use their voices to make sounds or tunes, though not words.

**6** Carry out a short vocal warm-up with the children.

**7** Practise with the children all they have learned so far by singing and rapping along to TRACK 17 – the backing track. This may be the first time they have sung along without the singing already being there for them, which will make things more challenging for them. They will have to make sure they know exactly where to come in, or it will all be out of time. Count properly the number of bars before they start singing and listen out for the musical phrase that leads you in.

**8** Ask the children how they think it is going. Are they improving each time? Are they enunciating the words properly so we can understand what they are singing?

**9** Practise the song again, correcting the mistakes made.

### Chill out time!

Have the children sit down at their desks. Each child should lay their head on their arms with eyes closed, breathing slowly through their nose. Ask them to think about their favourite feeling. Is it excitement? Is it calmness? Is it feeling powerful? Or just happy? What type of music would fit with their feeling? If they could pick any instrument, which one would they choose to play the music for that feeling? After a minute, get the children to put up their hands and say what they have imagined.

## **Lesson 6** The final rehearsal and performance

### Music objective

Practice of performance skills and final polishing of song.

### Learning activity

◆ Full vocal warm-up (QCA units 8:1 and 8:5).
◆ Practising the song (QCA unit 8:7).

### Learning activity

#### Unit 8 Ongoing skills

*'This unit focuses on the development of the singing voice and other essential musical skills (listening skills, aural memory and physical skills) that should be a regular part of classroom work week-by-week.'*
*'Singing songs with control and using the voice expressively.'*
Children should learn:

◆ Section 1 – to develop their singing voices.

◆ Section 5 – to recognise changes in, and control, pitch.

*'Listening, memory and movement.'*

◆ Section 7 – Children should learn to listen with attention to detail and develop aural memory.

#### Scottish attainment targets

*Expressing feelings, ideas, thought and solutions*

◆ Levels A–E – Invent music individually and in groups, displaying initiative and using knowledge of sound and structures gained in their explorations.

*Evaluating and appreciating*

◆ Level C – Give opinions of own music making and that of others and accept and offer suggestions for improvement.

## Lesson 6  *The final rehearsal and performance*

**1** 💿 Do a full vocal warm-up as described in lesson 1. Use the CD, TRACK 18, for a further vocal exercise, following the call and response.

**2** Next, work on some exercises for diction:

◆ Tell the children to imagine they have a pencil vertically in their mouth and to form a long 'aaaaah' sound.

◆ Tell them to imagine that they have a pencil horizontally in their mouth and to try to make a long 'eeeeh' sound.

◆ Now to do the 'funky gibbon'! Have the children stick their lips out into a pout and make a long 'oooooooh' sound.

◆ Encourage them to scrunch their face into a tight little ball for a few seconds then open out and make as big a face as possible, with a wide, open mouth and wide, open eyes.

◆ To exercise the tongue, have the children stick their tongues out and pretend their tongues are glued to their chins. Now, they should try speaking like that! Get them to say their names and addresses! (This usually amuses them.)

**3** Now, ask the children to speak through the words of the song as if they were talking through a window at somebody who couldn't hear them properly – to exaggerate the word shapes as if they were being lip-read. This is how they should sing the words of the song. It may feel odd, but it will sound right!

**4** Ask the children to sit down in two separate groups ready to practise performing: Group A should perform to Group B. Get the children to try to put the emotions of the song across. Are some of the words angry? (Parts of the rap perhaps?) Are some of the words sounding frightened? (The first verse perhaps?) Tell the performing group to look at the audience, stand up straight and sing the words with good diction!

**5** Ask Group B to give feedback to Group A – have the children put their hands up with their comments about the performance. You can help by asking them to comment about specific areas, for example:

◆ Do people know the words?

◆ Are they enunciating them properly so we can understand them?

◆ Was the singing loud enough?

## Lesson 6 *The final rehearsal and performance*

◆ Did the percussion break happen as planned?

◆ Did the rappers come in at the right place?

◆ Did the emotion of the song come across?

◆ How could it be improved?

◆ What went well and sounded good?

**6** Now swap over and repeat the process so that Group B performs to Group A, and Group A gives feedback.

**7** Take a little time now to practise any of the tricky sections before playing along to TRACK 17 again as a whole group.

**8** Practise the performance over TRACK 17 together. Ask if anyone has ideas about movement, choreography, or how you should stand as a group. Practise this now.

**9** The whole class should perform to the teacher, making sure they are standing up straight, looking out to the 'audience' and singing and enunciating loud and clear (without shouting).

Note: Remember to praise the children on how well they've done and how much they've achieved.

### Chill out time!

Have the children sit down at their desks. Each child should lay their head on their arms with eyes closed, breathing slowly through their nose. How do they feel (in their bodies and in their emotions)? Do they feel proud of what they've done? Ask them to sit and think about their feelings for a minute and then invite children to put their hands up to share any responses.

# Bully

**Verse 1**   Bully, bully, bully.
What d'you want from me today?
Bully, bully, bully.
My sandwich or my dinner money?
Bully, bully, bully.
You make my life a misery.
Scared to go to school today.
Coz you'll be there waiting for me.

**Verse 2**   Bully, bully, bully.
Why you doing this to me?
Bully, bully, bully.
Why are you so angry?
Bully, bully, bully.
Is someone hurting you this way?
Scared to go back home today?
Is someone gonna make you pay?

**Percussion break**

**Rap**   If you see someone shout and swear
And diss her name and what she wears
Don't just stand and watch and stare
Get some help, show that you care
BULLY – stop pulling her hair
BULLY – you're not being fair
BULLY – we're not impressed
BULLY – just give it a rest. Yo!

**Rap gap**

**Verse 3**   Bully, bully, bully.
You must be full of hate.
Bully, bully, bully.
Just stop and count to eight.
Bully, bully, bully.
Don't let this anger in.
Scared to show how small you feel,
Fight it and you can win.
Scared to show how small you feel,
Fight it and you can win.

**GOOD LUCK WITH YOUR PERFORMANCE!**
(Note: This performance can take place in the classroom, in front of the whole school at assembly, or as part of a school play. Wherever you perform it, make sure you all have fun doing it!)

© Folens (copiable page) Music Works Ages 7–9

# Lesson 1 The song: 'Senua da Dende'

## Music objective

Introducing the song, a two-part African round, and learning to sing it.

## Learning activity

◆ Doing a full vocal warm-up (QCA units 8:1 and 8:5).
◆ Learning basic techniques for building confidence in using the singing voice (QCA unit 8:1).
◆ Following and learning a new song in two parts (QCA units 8:4, 8:6 and 8:7).

## Learning activity

### Unit 8 Ongoing skills

*'This unit focuses on the development of the singing voice and other essential musical skills (listening skills, aural memory and physical skills) that should be a regular part of classroom work week-by-week.'*
*'Singing songs with control and using the voice expressively.'*
Children should learn:

◆ Section 1 – to develop their singing voices.
◆ Section 4 – to develop awareness of simple structures (phrases).
◆ Section 5 – to recognise changes in, and control, pitch.
◆ Section 6 – about how to express the meaning of songs.

*'Listening, memory and movement.'*

◆ Section 7 – Children should learn to listen with attention to detail and develop aural memory.

### Scottish attainment targets

*Evaluating and appreciating*
◆ Levels A–E – Demonstrate awareness of sound and responsiveness to music in a variety of styles.

*Using materials, techniques, skills and media (voice)*
◆ Level C – Sing confidently in unison, with some awareness of dynamics, phrasing and expression.

**1** 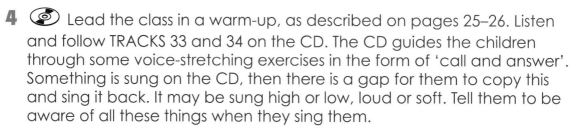 Tell the children to listen really carefully to the next song because you will be asking them questions about it. Play TRACK 31 on the CD – 'Senua da Dende'. Discuss the song with the children. Ask them to guess what language the song might be in and where the song might be from. Is the song old or new? Is the song cheerful or sad? Explain that the song is a Ghanaian folk song from Africa. It is very old and has been sung for many years. It is a traditional call-and-response song about a mother eagle and a baby eagle. The mother eagle is asking her little one to leave the nest, as (s)he is getting bigger and old enough to be on her or his own now.

**2** Have the whole class say together the phrase 'Senua da Dende senua'. Put the emphasis on the SEN of the 'Senua'. So, they should say it like this: **Sen**ua da dende, **Sen**ua. Count the pulse, 1,2,3,4 whilst the children are saying it. Note that the emphasised 'Sen's come on the '1', i.e. the first beat of the bar, which should always be emphasised slightly.

**3** Carry out a vocal warm-up. If needed, explain to the children that this stretches our vocal range so we learn to sing higher and lower than we could before. It also exercises the muscles we use to help make our voice strong. Ask the class where they think our voices come from. Most people will point to the throat or the mouth. Correct them: the voice just happens to pass through our vocal chords on the way out, but it needs the support of the whole body to do that. Vocal chords are too tiny and delicate to make the sound; they just help us to tune it. Explain that there are three things we need to make a nice loud singing sound:

- ◆ Big lungfuls of breath.
- ◆ A nice wide-open mouth to let the sound out.
- ◆ Using the whole body, especially our tummy muscles, to support the sound.

**4**  Lead the class in a warm-up, as described on pages 25–26. Listen and follow TRACKS 33 and 34 on the CD. The CD guides the children through some voice-stretching exercises in the form of 'call and answer'. Something is sung on the CD, then there is a gap for them to copy this and sing it back. It may be sung high or low, loud or soft. Tell them to be aware of all these things when they sing them.

**5** Listen to TRACK 31 on the CD again. Can the children hear the call and then the response? The response doesn't wait for the call to finish completely – it interrupts it just before it has finished by starting on the last 'senua'. Listen to TRACK 32 on the CD. This is the tune sung on its own, without the response. Point out that there are four musical phrases. The first two are the same – they both go down in steps. The third is longer. It starts higher up and then travels down in steps. The fourth phrase is similar in length to the first but with a slightly different tune – ask the children if they can hear it.

**6** Listen to TRACK 35 on the CD. Each of the four musical phrases is sung with a gap for the children to sing back exactly the same. There's a pulse underneath so that the children stay in time. Repeat this process a few times until the children all feel familiar with the tune.

**7** Now sing along to TRACK 36. This is the whole four phrases of the tune sung without the 'answer'. Practise singing this straight through with the class. Clap the pulse to help them stay in time.

**8** Now split the class into two equal groups. Try the round without the help of the CD. Explain that the second group starts after the first group has sung 'Senua da dende...' They come in on the last 'Senua' with the start of the tune. Explain how tricky it can be to do this! They are singing different rhythms and tunes at the same time. (It's like rubbing your stomach whilst patting your head.) Clap the pulse whilst singing too. Try swapping the groups round so that the group that went second has a chance to start this time.

**Chill out time!**

Have the children sit down at their desks. Each child should lay their head on their arms with eyes closed, breathing slowly through their nose. Ask them to listen to the sounds around them in silence. After one minute, ask them to put up their hands and say what they've heard.

**Lesson 2** *Adding rhythms*

*Note – You will be using the percussion trolley for this lesson.*

## Music objective

Recapping the song; learning percussion parts.

## Learning activity

◆ Doing a warm-up (QCA units 8:1 and 8:5).

◆ Building confidence in using the singing voice and singing in parts (QCA units 8:2, 8:3 and 8:4).

◆ Learning simple percussion parts (QCA units 10:1 and 10:2).

## Learning activity

### Unit 8 Ongoing skills

*'This unit focuses on the development of the singing voice and other essential musical skills (listening skills, aural memory and physical skills) that should be a regular part of classroom work week-by-week.'*
*'Singing songs with control and using the voice expressively.'*
Children should learn:

◆ Section 1 – to develop their singing voices.

◆ Section 2 – to use the thinking voice (internalising).

◆ Section 4 – to develop awareness of simple structures (phrases).

◆ Section 5 – to recognise changes in, and control, pitch.

### Unit 10 Exploring rhythmic patterns

*'In this unit, children extend their understanding of rhythmic patterns, and in particular, ostinato. They create their own patterns and play them separately and in combination with other patterns. They identify repeated patterns in different types of music.'*
Children should learn:

◆ Section 1 – about repeated rhythmic patterns.

◆ Section 2 – about rhythmic patterns; how rhythms can be described through rhythmic symbols (notation).

### Scottish attainment targets

*Using materials, techniques, skills and media (instruments)*

◆ Level A – Use basic playing techniques such as shaking and tapping, keeping the beat and repeating simple rhythmic patterns.

◆ Level B – Play simple rhythmic parts, showing some control over speed and volume in response to simple signals of direction.

# Lesson 2 ) Adding rhythms

1  🔘 Play TRACKS 31 and 32 on the CD – 'Senua da Dende' – to remind the children of the song and the way the rounds work.

2  Ask children to put their hands up if they remember what the song is about and where it is from.

3  Practise the words 'Senua da dende' with the children. Tell them to just say the words in the rhythm they are sung in, remembering to emphasise the SEN of 'Senua'.

4  Get the children to clap along with the rhythm of the words. Once the children are familiar with it, ask them to not say the words, but just to clap the rhythm. Rhythm is different to pulse – pulse stays steady throughout the whole song and the gaps are spaced evenly between each beat; with rhythm, the gaps vary.

5  Next remind the children of the tune. Sing the song all together in one part. (Note: the key of C is a good one for this song; the starting note is G. If you don't have a piano handy, you can get it on the recorder by holding thumb and top three fingers down.)

6  Split the class into two and start at different times, doing the song as a round, just as you did in the last lesson. Swap the groups over.

7  🔘 Listen to TRACK 37 on the CD. This is the pulse of the song. Ask the children to clap the pulse and sing the song in unison. See how the pulse stays the same throughout the song. They can count '1, 2, 3, 4, 1, 2, 3, 4...' along with the pulse and put emphasis on the 1 as they clap. This first beat of the bar should always be louder than the others.

8  Get half the class to clap the rhythm of the words, whilst the rest does the steady pulse. Swap over. Ask them which part is easiest to do and if it is difficult to keep the pulse steady with the rhythm going on as well.

9  🔘 Listen to TRACK 38 on the CD. This is a simple percussion part to accompany the song. Ask the class to clap along to this new rhythm.

**10** Now split the class into two. One group should clap the pulse whilst the other claps the new rhythm. Once they have successfully done this, then swap the groups round.

**11** Keep the class in two groups (A and B). Group A will play the pulse and Group B will play the rhythm. These groups should also be used for the two parts of the round.

**12** Give out percussion from the trolley. (You could try giving all the woodblocks to the pulse group and all the shakers and tambourines to the rhythm group, but any mixed percussion will work.) Start Group A off with the pulse and, once they are established, add Group B with the rhythm.

**13** Now practise singing through 'Senua' in unison whilst playing the percussion.

**14** Now sing and play along with TRACK 31 on the CD, singing the round, then adding the percussion break, which goes under the rap.

## Chill out time!

Ask the children to sit down at their desks. Each child should lay their head on their arms with eyes closed, breathing slowly through their nose. Ask them to go through the song in their heads, without saying anything. Can they hear the two parts of the round? Can they imagine the rhythms as well? This is using their 'thinking voice', i.e. they are hearing the song in their heads without singing it, like reading a book without speaking the words. After a couple of minutes, ask them how this was for them.

# Lesson 3   The rap

*Note – You will be using the percussion trolley for this lesson.*

## Music objective

Learning the rap section and writing their own rap for the rap section (i.e. creating rhythmic verse matching words with meter) on the theme of being too old or too young.

## Learning activity

◆ Learning the rap section in the song (QCA units 8:4 and 8:7).

◆ Creating a series of (possibly) rhyming phrases that fit with the pulse of the song, so creating a rap (QCA unit 10:4).

◆ Practising this rap along with the percussion and the rest of the song (QCA units 8:4 and 8:7).

## Learning activity

### Unit 8 Ongoing skills

*'This unit focuses on the development of the singing voice and other essential musical skills (listening skills, aural memory and physical skills) that should be a regular part of classroom work week-by-week.'*
*'Singing songs with control and using the voice expressively.'*

◆ Section 4 – Children should learn to develop awareness of simple structures (phrases).

*'Listening, memory and movement.'*

◆ Section 7 – Children should learn to listen with attention to detail and develop aural memory.

### Unit 10 Exploring rhythmic patterns

*'In this unit, children extend their understanding of rhythmic patterns, and in particular, ostinato. They create their own patterns and play them separately and in combination with other patterns. They identify repeated patterns in different types of music.'*
*'Bringing it all together.'*

◆ Section 4 – Children should learn to compose music using rhythmic ostinati based on spoken phrase.

 **Scottish attainment targets**

*Using materials, techniques, skills and media (voice)*

◆ Level B – Show a greater ability to sing in tune with others; control rhythm, speed and leaps in melody.

◆ Level C – Sing together confidently in unison.

**1** Play the song on the CD (TRACK 31) and ask the children to clap to the pulse.

**2** Listen to the rap section of the CD (TRACK 39).

**3** Discussion time. The theme of the song is about how children sometimes feel they are told they are too young to do some things (like stay up late to watch a film), but old enough now to do things they would rather not (for example, tidying their room, doing dishes)! Get the children to come up with some examples. What do their parents/guardians/teachers say they are too young for? What do their parents and so on say they are old enough to do now? Write these examples up on the board. How do the children feel about this? Does it feel fair? What rules would they make for themselves? What rules would they make if they were the parents?

**4** Pick out as a team what you definitely want to include in your rap and circle these on the board.

**5** With the class, clap along to the rhythm of the words of the existing rap. Use this rhythm to try to fit in some of the phrases the class have chosen. You may have to adapt them – lengthen, shorten and so on – to fit with the pulse. Ask the children to think of relevant words that rhyme with some of the phrases that you have chosen. Arrange them in a fitting order.

**6** There's a gap for the rap in the track. After they hear 'That means I'm way too old to go to bed at eight' the children should come in with their new rap, keeping to the pulse. Does it fit, or is it too long or short? Ask them to cut it down or add to it as required. Do they want to keep the class split in two and split some parts of the rap up? Have fun experimenting as much as you want!

**7** Practise your rap. (Clapping the pulse will help you to rap in time.)

**8** Now the children should practise the rap whilst playing their percussion. Split the children into the two percussion/singing groups. Get the pulse going first then add the rhythm. Say the whole rap through over the percussion.

**9** Practise right through from the beginning of the pre-written rap section.

**10**  Now practise right from the beginning of the song. Use the recording (TRACK 31) to help you if you need it.

**11** Ask if any of the children would like to perform the rap to the rest of the class – use TRACK 37 for this. They could perform in small groups of about three or four, if they prefer.

## Chill out time!

Have the children sit down at their desks. Each child should lay their head on their arms with eyes closed, breathing slowly through their nose. The children have had a good old moan about all the things that aren't fair; now it's time to think of all the good things their parents and teachers have done for them. Ask them to think of all the fun times they've had, times when they felt really lucky or special because of a parent or teacher. After a few minutes of contemplation, invite children to volunteer to share their thoughts.

**Lesson 4** *Singing games*

## Music objective

Adding to the song by turning it into a singing game.

## Learning activity

◆ Exploring singing games (QCA unit 14:2).

◆ Changing the song words to use as a singing game (QCA unit 14:4).

◆ Recapping the song and rhythms (QCA units 8:1, 8:4–6 and 8:7).

## Learning activity

### Unit 14 Salt, pepper, vinegar, mustard – Exploring singing games

*'This unit develops children's ability to recognise and explore some characteristics of singing games. It consolidates their sense of pulse and ability to perform with others.'*
*'What are the characteristics of singing games?'*

◆ Section 2 – Children should learn that singing games have specific musical and other characteristics that contribute to their success.

*'Can we make up our own playground singing games and songs?'*

◆ Section 4 – Children should learn how to make up their own singing games and add appropriate actions.

### Unit 8 Ongoing skills

*'This unit focuses on the development of the singing voice and other essential musical skills (listening skills, aural memory and physical skills) that should be a regular part of classroom work week-by-week.'*
*'Singing songs with control and using the voice expressively.'*
Children should learn:

◆ Section 1 – to develop their singing voices.

◆ Section 4 – to develop awareness of simple structures (phrases).

◆ Section 5 – to recognise changes in, and control, pitch.

◆ Section 6 – about how to express the meaning of songs.

*'Listening, memory and movement.'*

◆ Section 7 – Children should learn to listen with attention to detail and develop aural memory.

 Scottish attainment targets

*Using materials, techniques, skills and media (investigating: exploring sound)*

◆ Level C – Experiment with different combinations and qualities of sound to represent contrasting moods and effects.

# **Lesson 4** *Singing games*

**1** Explain to the children that a singing game is a song that has actions that accompany it, for example, skipping, clapping, joining hands and so on. They are always very repetitive and catchy. Ask them which singing games they know.

**2** Ask one or two children to come to the front of the class and perform a singing game for the others to watch. Allow another group to have a go as well. Make a list on the board of all the singing games the class can think of and discuss what actions go with them. What different sorts of actions can go with a singing game?

**3** Now challenge the children to turn 'Senua da Dende' into a singing game. To begin with, they can change the words but not the tune. Ask them to sing through the song in unison as it is, to remind them of the tune and rhythm. Then split the class into two groups and perform as a round. Now, change the words to 'I want a bowl of Frosties!' and sing to the same tune, coming in with the second part at the same point in the tune as usual. So, the whole single melody line would be – 'I want a bowl of Frosties, I want a bowl of Frosties, I want a bowl of, I want a bowl of, I want a bowl of Frosties!'

**4** Do the children have any other ideas? Remind them the theme of the song is about children growing older and being too young for some things but too old for others. Get them to clap the rhythm of the words. Any new words should have the same rhythm – for example, 'Bring me a cup of coffee', 'I feel like watching telly', or 'Teacher says we're too noisy!'

**5** 'Senua' is a call-and-response song, so the next step is to have the first group doing the call, and the second group replying with their answer. So, you have to come up with a second line of words. Get the class to put hands up with ideas and write them all on the board. Examples could be 'Bring me a cup of coffee. I'm busy eating toffee' or 'Teacher says we're too noisy. We think that she's too bossy'. Perhaps one line could be a parent and the other the child's response, or the other way around. Try to stick to the theme. (Note: Make sure that you choose to end the first line with a word that has a good choice of rhymes! Also, the rhymes don't have to be exact.)

**6** Try singing a couple of different suggestions that you think would work. (Note: The children will be singing different words together on the third and fourth lines, so this will make it trickier for them.) Once you are happy with your choice, then practise until the children are familiar with it.

**7** Next, put some actions to the best words that they have written. Get children to come up with their own ideas. Some suggestions are:

- ◆ Using the content of their words to suggest certain actions: for example, eating a bowl of cereal.

- ◆ Working in pairs, doing the song as a clapping game, with each partner singing the call and response to each other. (Note: this is tricky as each person is singing their part solo.)

- ◆ Separating the two halves of the class to call and respond and do an action such as moving towards the other group wagging a finger when the line is being sung, moving away when the other half comes near.

- ◆ Singing in two chains, weaving through each other.

**8** Choose one of the games to perform as an extra section in the song. It should go after the 'Senua da dende' section that follows on after the raps. You may decide to just have a few children doing the singing game whilst the rest carry on with the percussion. The whole class might do it, but remember they will have to contend with their percussion instruments! (Perhaps some children could clap their rhythm rather than use an instrument.) Solve these issues together.

**9** Practise your chosen singing game in context. So, split the class into two, clap rather then use percussion instruments, and sing through two rounds of 'Senua', going straight into the singing game then straight back into two rounds of 'Senua' again. Try to get the transition as smooth as possible!

## Chill out time!

Have the children sit down at their desks. Each child should lay their head on their arms with eyes closed, breathing slowly through their nose. Tell them they're going to relax after all that activity, and that they should feel their bodies relax into their chairs and onto the desks. Ask them to slowly breathe in right down from their diaphragms and fill their lungs up GENTLY to the top, then to sigh out quietly on the out-breath. Remind them to feel the chair and desk supporting their weight and let themselves sink onto them. Let them relax quietly for a short time.

## Lesson 5 — Painting with sound

*Note – You will be using the instrument trolley for this lesson.*
*You will also need:*
◆ *A picture of a sunrise (in the countryside)*
◆ *A picture of a busy city*
◆ *A picture of a billowy sea*
*(Note: These can be photographs or paintings.)*

### Music objective

Identifying different moods with different pieces of music; creating musical pictures; recapping the song.

### Learning activity

◆ Listening to three contrasting pieces of music and identifying which pictures they portray (QCA units 13:1, 13:2 and 13:4).
◆ Creating their own musical pictures (QCA units 13:1, 13:2 and 13:4).

### Learning activity

**Unit 13 Painting with sound – Exploring sound colours**
*'This unit develops children's ability to create, perform and analyse expressive compositions and extend their sound vocabulary.'*
*'How can music describe images and moods?'*
◆ Section 1 – Children should learn that music, like pictures, can describe images and moods.
*'How can we use sounds to create a picture or mood?'*
Children should learn:
◆ Section 2 – to relate sounds to visual images; to select appropriate instruments.
◆ Section 4 – how mood and emotion can be illustrated in music.

**Scottish attainment targets**
*Using materials, techniques, skills and media (investigating: exploring sound)*
◆ Level C – Experiment with different combinations and qualities of sound to represent contrasting moods and effects.

**Lesson 5** *Painting with sound*

**1** Show the children your three different pictures of the sunrise, cityscape and the sea. Tell the children they will be listening to three different pieces of music and to see if they can work out which one represents which picture. Now listen to TRACKS 40, 41 and 42.

**2** Ask the children to 'vote' on which piece of music went with which picture. (TRACK 40 is the sunrise, 41 the cityscape and 42 is the sea.)

**3** Use these questions to prompt the children's thoughts:
- Why did the pieces of music sound different?
- Why did that music remind us of the sunrise?
- Was the piece slow or fast?
- What instruments were used?
- Were they short sounds or long, held sounds?
- What instruments made us think of a busy city?
- Was it played quickly or slowly?
- Were they short sounds or long sounds?
- What about the stormy sea?
- Did the music go in 'waves'?
- Did the volume of the music go up and down like waves?

**4** Split the class into three groups and assign them one of the pictures each.

**5** Pick instruments from the trolley and get each group to create a short musical piece describing their picture using tuned and untuned instruments, for example, try:

- The sunrise – gently and very slowly play notes, going up in pitch on the chime bars, glockenspiel or xylophone representing the slow rise of the sun and gradual lightening of the sky. No percussion. Long-held, high-pitched recorder notes. The tempo could gradually increase.

- Busy cityscape – woodblocks and any other percussion. People playing at different tempos suggesting busyness and frenetic activity. Some people playing fast rhythms, some slow. (Don't have everyone playing frenetically fast as it will sound too chaotic!) Use horn noises for car horns, fast shakers and cowbells. Children could use voices to perhaps repeat a sound such as a police car.

## Lesson 5 ) *Painting with sound*

◆ Billowing sea – use maracas and tambourines to get the children to work together in 'waves' of sound like the waves of the sea, increasing in volume and frequency with each wave, then receding until the next one. They need to feel the waves together.

**6** Once the children have had enough time to practise separately, then ask each group to perform their piece to the class, displaying the picture prominently as they play. Did it work? Give feedback and praise!

**7** 💿 Now listen to TRACKS 33 and 34 on the CD for a quick vocal warm-up.

**8** Split into two groups and hand out the percussion instruments. Talk through the song together, reminding them of the rhythms, the words, the rap section and the singing game.

**9** 💿 Practise right from the beginning of the song. Use the recording (TRACK 31) to help you if you need it. (Note: The recording obviously won't have your singing game on it. It stops just before you start the singing-game section and you will have to do the singing game and last round of 'Senua's on your own.)

### Chill out time!

Have the children sit down at their desks. Each child should lay their head on their arms with eyes closed, breathing slowly through their nose. Do the same relaxation exercise as the last lesson, but this time get them to think of being 'in' either the sunset, the city or the sea picture – it's their choice. Afterwards, invite them to comment on their thoughts to see how their feelings compare.

# Lesson 6 The final rehearsal and performance

## Music objective

Practice of performance skills and final polishing of song.

## Learning activity

◆ Full vocal warm-up (QCA units 8:1 and 8:5).

◆ Practising the song (QCA unit 8:7).

◆ Performing the song to each other (QCA unit 11:7).

◆ Giving constructive feedback to each other (QCA unit 11:7).

## Learning activity

### Unit 8 Ongoing skills

*'This unit focuses on the development of the singing voice and other essential musical skills (listening skills, aural memory and physical skills) that should be a regular part of classroom work week-by-week.'*
*'Singing songs with control and using the voice expressively.'*
Children should learn:

◆ Section 1 – to develop their singing voices.

◆ Section 5 – to recognise changes in, and control, pitch.

*'Listening, memory and movement.'*

◆ Section 7 – Children should learn to listen with attention to detail and develop aural memory.

### Unit 11 The class orchestra – Exploring arrangements

*'This unit develops children's ability to create, combine and perform rhythmic and melodic material as part of a class performance of a song.'*
*'Bringing it all together: let's arrange our own song.'*

◆ Section 7 – Children should learn how to present a class performance.

###  Scottish attainment targets

*Using materials, techniques, skills and media (investigating: exploring sound)*

◆ Level C – Experiment with different combinations and qualities of sound to represent contrasting moods and effects.

**Lesson 6** *The final rehearsal and performance*

**1** Do a full vocal warm-up as described in lesson 1.

**2** Next, try some fun exercises to practise diction:

◆ The children should say 'pizza' slowly and in an exaggerated way, like 'Peeeeezaaaaaaaaah', making their mouths go as wide as possible on the 'eeeee' sound and as vertically big as possible on the 'aaaaah' sound.

◆ Now do the 'funky gibbon'! Have the children stick their lips out into a pout and make a long 'ooooooooh' sound.

◆ Now ask them to say 'Satsuma', exaggerating the tall 'aaaaah' shape and pouting for the 'ooooh': 'Saaatsoooooooooomaaaaah'.

◆ Have some fun trying out some of your suggestions, for example, 'weetabix', exaggerating each vowel.

◆ 'Senua' has a lot of 's' sounds in it, so together try slowly and exaggeratedly 'She sells sea shells on the sea shore'.

◆ Now ask the children to speak through the words of the song as if they were talking through a window at somebody who couldn't hear them properly. They have to exaggerate the word shapes as if they were being lip-read. This is how they should sing the words of the song. It may feel odd, but it will sound right!

**3** Talk through the order of the song with the class. Point out that it's a very complex arrangement – they will sing 'Senua' twice through, then the rap, then their own rap, then 'Senua' twice through, then the singing game, then 'Senua' twice through to finish.

**4** Practise the song all the way through together without the backing track. Just concentrate on getting everything in the right order this time. (Remember the start note is G.)

**5** How did it go? Discuss together. See if the children can make any comments on improvements that could be made.

**6** Once the 'nuts and bolts' of the song are in place (the order, the words and so on) you are ready to practise performing. Split the class into two, with a mixture of call and answer people in both. Group A should now perform to Group B. (Note: you may have to miss out parts of the singing game for this.) Encourage them to look at the audience, stand up straight and sing the words with good diction!

## Lesson 6 — *The final rehearsal and performance*

**7** Group B should give feedback to the Group A. Ask others to put their hands up with their comments about the performance. Ask them to comment about specific areas, for example,

- ◆ Nuts and bolts: Do people know the words? Do people know the order? Was the timing right? Was the tuning right?

- ◆ Performing issues: Was the singing loud enough? Did they enunciate the words properly so we could understand them? How could it be improved? What went well and sounded good?

**8** Now swap over and repeat the process, with Group B performing to Group A, and Group A giving feedback.

**9** Practise any individual bits that need addressing.

**10** Lastly, have the whole class perform to the teacher, making sure they are standing up straight, looking out to the 'audience' and singing and enunciating loud and clear (without shouting). Note: Remember to praise the children on how well they've done and how much they've achieved.

### Chill out time!

Have the children sit down at their desks. Each child should lay their head on their arms with eyes closed, breathing slowly through their nose. They should relax into their bodies and slow their breathing down. Get them to think back and remember the whole journey of learning and writing the song. They should try to remember each lesson and what they learned and how much of the song they've written themselves. Do they feel proud of what they've done? Get them to sit with their thoughts and feelings for a minute and then encourage volunteers to put their hands up if they'd like to share their responses.

# Senua da Dende
*(traditional song from Ghana)*

**Chorus**   Senua da dende senua
Senua da dende senua
Senua da dende
Senua da dende
Senua da dende senua (all x 3)

**Rap\***   Mamma says I'm old enough now to help her do the dishes.
I say – I'm old enough now to follow my own wishes.
My mamma says I'm old enough to start to pull my weight.
That means I'm way too old to go to bed at eight.

**Rap gap**

**GOOD
LUCK WITH YOUR
PERFORMANCE!**
*(Note: This performance
can take place in the
classroom, in front of the whole
school at assembly, or as part
of a school play. Wherever
you perform it, make
sure you all have fun
doing it!)*

**Chorus**   Senua da dende senua
Senua da dende senua
Senua da dende
Senua da dende
Senua da dende senua (all x 2)

(\* The rap isn't traditional Ghanaian!)

# Friendship

# Bully

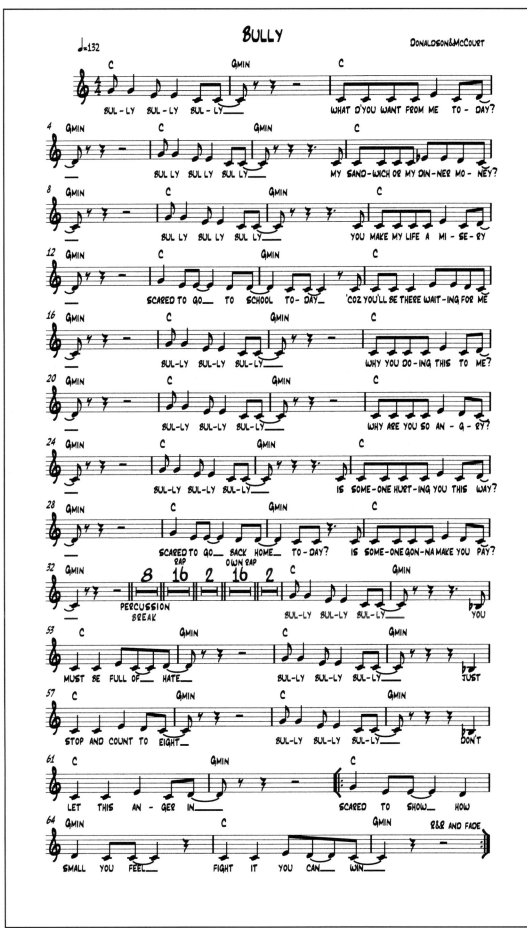

# Senua da Dende

# Friendship

Make a friendship bracelet! Make a bracelet for your friend by threading pasta tubes onto some string or elastic. You can paint it and decorate it in a way your friend will like.

Get into pairs and draw a picture of your friend. If you are being the model, you have to sit *really* still to let your friend draw you. If you are being the artist, look at your friend very carefully so you can be sure of catching all the details of their face.

© Folens (copiable page) Music Works Ages 7–9

# Friendship

With the rest of the class, discuss some ideas of how you could be 'friends of the earth'. Some issues to think about are litter, global warming, pollution and deforestation. Pick one of the issues that you found important and design a poster to encourage other children to help create a friendly earth.

Listen to your teacher read the story of the Good Samaritan from the Bible (Luke 10: 25–37). Can you think where a similar story might happen today? With your group, make up a short play to show a modern-day Good Samaritan.

# Bullying

In your pairs or small groups, make a list of things you think are acts of bullying. Not all bullying is obvious, remember – sometimes it could be not including someone in a game, or ignoring them. Choose one of the points on your list and act it out with your group for the rest of the class. Your teacher will ask you to 'freeze' and then get the other children in the class to comment on how the different people might be feeling, or how the situation could be resolved.

# Bullying

Design a game you could play with your friends – it could be any kind, such as a board game or a new game to play in the playground. Think of the rules and guidelines you would need so that the game could be played fairly. Share your new game with the rest of the class and explain the rules – perhaps you could play it at break time!